*Make sure your memories will last a lifetime!*

Journal dates:

_____

to

_____

date:

date:

> I am still determined to be cheerful and happy in whatever situation I may be.
>
> — Martha Washington

date:

date:

> I have taught you in the way of wisdom; I have led you in right paths. When you walk, your steps will not be hindered, And when you run, you will not stumble.
>
> Proverbs 4:11-12

cdef

date: _____

> Undertake not what you cannot perform, but be careful to keep your promise.
> — *Life of George Washington*

date: _____

> It is to me a most affecting thing to hear myself prayed for, in particular as I do every day in the week, and disposes me to bear with more composure, some disagreeable circumstances that attend my situation.
>
> — John Adams

date:

Do not be wise in your own eyes;
Fear the LORD and depart from evil.

— Solomon

date:

> Repay no one evil for evil. Have regard for good things in the sight of all men. If it is possible, as much as depends on you, live peaceably with all men.
>
> Romans 12: 17-18

date:

cdef

date: _____

> I rejoice in my son,
> who always speaks the truth.
> — Mary Ball Washington,
> mother of
> Gen. George Washington

date:

JOURNAL

> His loved wife kneeled beside his bed, with her head resting on the Bible, which she daily read the precepts, and cheering promises of her Saviour; and they comforted her in her hour of deepest sorrow.
>
> — Life of George Washington

date:

But I will hope continually,
And will praise You yet more
and more.

— King David

date:

rstuv

> Well, knowledge is a fine thing, and mother Eve thought so; but she smarted so severely for hers, that most of her daughters have been afraid of it since.
>
> — Abigail Adams

date:

cdef

date: _____

> God has set before me, as my object, the reformation of my country's manners.
> — William Wilberforce

date:

# JOURNAL

> She never omitted her private devotions or her public duties; and she and her husband were so perfectly united and happy that he must have been a Christian.
>
> — the grandaughter of Martha Washington, wife of George Washington

date:

date:

Hope deferred makes the heart sick, But when the desire comes, it is a tree of life.

— Solomon

date:

> They began with prayer, and ended in victory and thanksgiving.
>
> — Anna Reed, author of *Life of George Washington*, honoring America's patriots

cdef

I hope you will have good sense enough to disregard those foolish predictions that the world is to be at an end soon. The Almighty has never made known to any body at what time he created it; nor will he tell any body when he will put an end to it, if he ever means to do it. As to preparations for that event, the best way is for you always to be prepared for it. The only way to be so is, never say or do a bad thing. If ever you are about to say any thing amiss, or to do any thing wrong, consider beforehand; you will feel something within you which will tell you it is wrong, and ought not to be said or done. This is your conscience, and be sure and obey it. Our Maker has given us this faith internal monitor, and if you always obey it you will always be prepared for the end of the world; or for a much more certain event, which is death. This must happen to all; it puts an end to the world as to us; and the way to be ready for it is never to do a wrong act.

— Thomas Jefferson to his daughter Martha,
Dec. 11, 1783

date:

# JOURNAL

> You will say then, "Branches were broken off that I might be grafted in." Well said. Because of unbelief they were broken off, and you stand by faith. Do not be haughty, but fear. For if God did not spare the natural branches, He may not spare you either.
>
> Romans 11:19-21

date:

When you speak of God, or his attributes, let it be seriously in reverence.

— *Life of George Washington*

date:

> I have no ambition to govern men.
> It is a painful and thankless office.
> — Thomas Jefferson to John Adams

date:

cdef

date:

> Let the hospitalities of the house with respect to the poor be kept up. Let no one go hungry away.
> — Gen. George Washington

date:

JOURNA

> Every good gift and every perfect gift is from above, and comes down from the Father of lights, with whom there is no variation or shadow of turning. Of His own will He brought us forth by the word of truth, that we might be a kind of firstfruits of His creatures.
>
> — James 1:17-18

date: _____

> To be good, and do good, is the whole duty of man comprised in a few words.
>
> — Abigail Adams

date:

date:

> Woman pray for me! Thus in that hour when the soul feels what it truly is, and that soon it must be in the presence of its holy Creator and just Judge, the duty and value of prayer is owned.
> — *Life of George Washington*

date:

cdef

date:

> Behold, the eye of the LORD is on those who fear Him, On those who hope in His mercy.
> – King David

date:

date: _____

I have travelled far now on life's journey; and, having climbed one of the few remaining hills between earth and Heaven, I stand awhile on this vantage-ground, and look back across the country through which the Lord has led me....

I can see two pilgrims treading this highway of life together, hand in hand, heart linked to heart. True, they have had rivers to ford, and mountains to cross, and fierce enemies to fight, and many dangers to go through; but their Guide was watchful, their Deliverer unfailing, and of them it might truly be said, "In all their affliction He was afflicted, and the Angel of His presence saved them; in His love and in His pity He redeemed them; and He bare them, and carried them all the days of old."

All this I see in retrospect...and if, seeing how unspeakably good the Lord has been to me, you should be led to love Him more, and serve Him better, and trust Him more fully, I shall have abundant reason to bless Him for giving me **TEN YEARS AFTER!**

— Susannah Spurgeon, *Ten Years After*

date:

The lips of the righteous feed many,
But fools die for lack of wisdom. The
blessing of the LORD makes one rich,
And He adds no sorrow with it.
— Solomon

date:

> But let all those rejoice who put their trust in You; Let them ever shout for joy, because You defend them; Let those also who love Your name Be joyful in You.
>
> — King David

cdef

date: _____

> LORD, I hope for Your salvation,
> And I do Your commandments.
> — King David

date:

date:

# JOURNAL

> I had anticipated from that moment we should be suffered to grow old together in solitude and tranquility. That was the first and dearest wish of my life.
>
> — Martha Washington
> on Gen. Washington's retirement from public life

date:

For as the body without the spirit is dead, so faith without works is dead also.

— James 2:26

date:

> Her miniature portrait was found on the bosom of Washington, where he had worn it for forty years.
>
> — Gen. Washington's devotion to his wife Martha until his death

cdef

date: _____

I have taught you in the way of wisdom; I have led you in right paths. When you walk, your steps will not be hindered, And when you run, you will not stumble.

— Solomon

date:

JOURNAL

> I have also learned from experience, that the greater part of our happiness or misery depends on our dispositions, and not our circumstances. We carry the seeds of the one or the other about with us in our minds wherever we go.
>
> — Martha Washington

date:

date:

Bless those who persecute you; bless and do not curse. Rejoice with those who rejoice, and weep with those who weep.

Romans 12: 14-15

date:

rstuv

> You can easily distinguish him when Congress goes to prayers - Mr. Washington is the gentleman who kneels down.
>
> — *Life of George Washington*

cdef

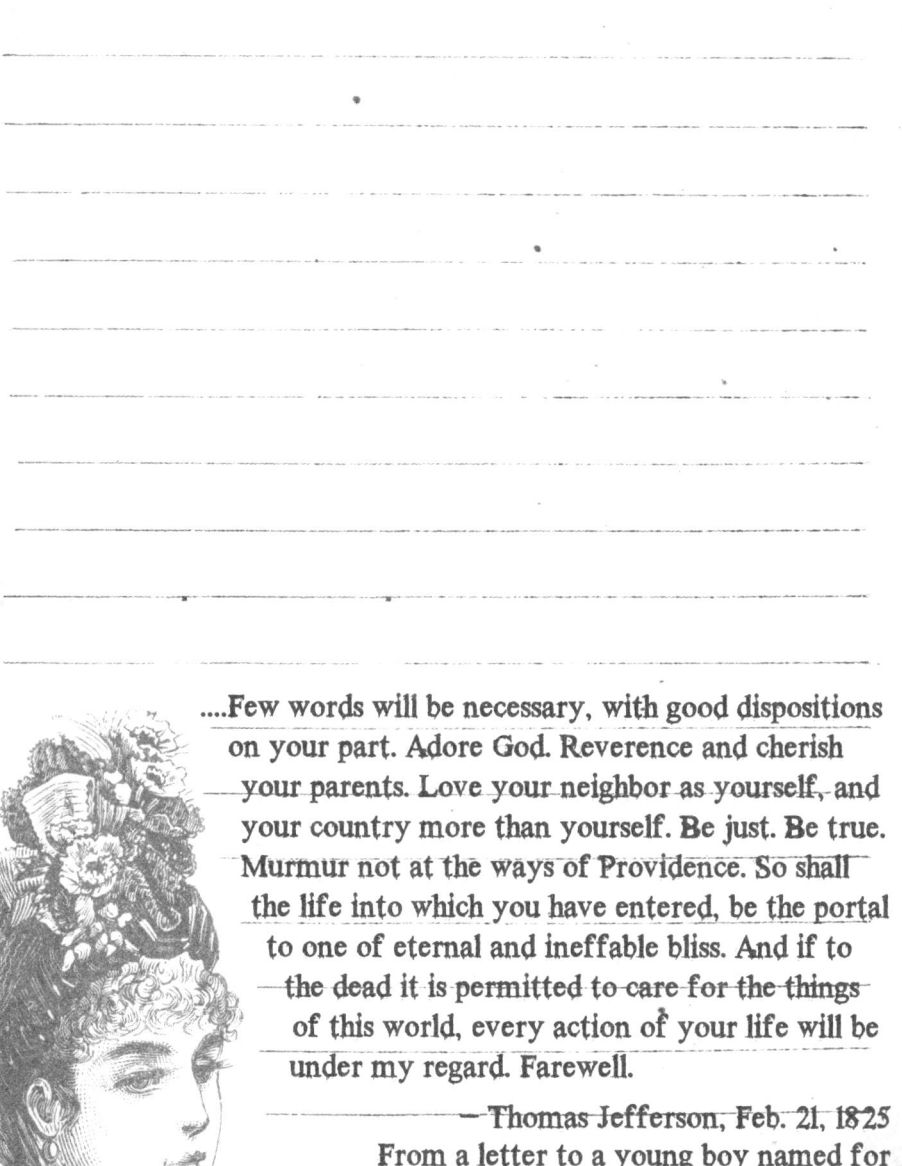

....Few words will be necessary, with good dispositions on your part. Adore God. Reverence and cherish your parents. Love your neighbor as yourself, and your country more than yourself. Be just. Be true. Murmur not at the ways of Providence. So shall the life into which you have entered, be the portal to one of eternal and ineffable bliss. And if to the dead it is permitted to care for the things of this world, every action of your life will be under my regard. Farewell.

—Thomas Jefferson, Feb. 21, 1825
From a letter to a young boy named for Jefferson written at the child's father's request

date:

# JOURNAL

> No doubt many pious American hearts offered such a prayer, with humility and faith and their prayers were granted; for they never would have succeeded in defending their rights, unless the mighty hand of God had upheld and guided them.
>
> — Anna Reed, author of *Life of George Washington*

date:

Speak not injurious words, neither in jest nor earnest; scoff at none, although they give occasion.

— *Life of George Washington*

date: _____

date:

> See the wondrous works of Providence,
> and the uncertainty of human things.
>
> — *Life of George Washington*

cdef

date:

> Great necessities
> call out great virtues.
> — Abigail Adams

date:

First printing: September 2011

Copyright © 2011 by Attic Books. All rights reserved. No part of this book may be used or reproduced in any manner whatsoever without written permission of the publisher, except in the case of brief quotations in articles and reviews. For information write:

Attic Books, P.O. Box 726, Green Forest, AR 72638

Attic Books is a division of the New Leaf Publishing Group, Inc.

ISBN: 978-0-89051-629-4

Cover by Justin Skinner

Unless otherwise noted, Scripture quotations are from the New King James Version of the Bible.

Printed in China

Please visit our website for other great titles:
www.attic-books.net